Madeleine Dring

Seven Shakespeare Songs

For medium voice and piano

The Cuckoo

It was a lover

Take O take those lips away

Under the greenwood tree*

Come away, death*

Blow, blow thou winter wind*

Crabbed age and youth

*Reprinted by kind permission of Alfred Lengnick and Co Ltd.

A Thames publication

EXCLUSIVELY DISTRIBUTED BY

HAL•LEONARD®

Madeleine Dring

Madeleine Dring was born in 1923 and from an early age showed precocious musical talent. She was encouraged by her parents, who were both good amateur musicians, and won a junior violin scholarship to the Royal College of Music in London when only ten. She also studied piano and singing, and it was at this time that her love for the theatre developed: she had the opportunity to write music for the children's plays put on by the RCM Junior Department, as well as to act in them. On leaving school she won two more scholarships and became a full-time senior student at the college, adding composition to her studies.

The piano was her favoured instrument; she played brilliantly and enjoyed writing for it, composing a solo sonata and many shorter pieces. In the late 1940s and early 1950s there was a vogue for two-piano music - particularly useful in accompanying the intimate revues so popular at that period - and she found this a very pleasing idiom. Her love of the dance was expressed in this keyboard music - the flavour of the Caribbean, the syncopation of jazz, the nostalgia of Paris, the excitement of the tarantella.

Her feeling for style was of great value when it came to the setting of words. Shakespeare and Herrick were two of her favourites, but 20th-century poets were not excluded; her Betjeman settings (published in 1980 by Weinberger) are perhaps the best-known of her songs. These Betjeman settings, however, number only five out of an output of over 50, and that excludes her cabaret and theatre material. From student days in the early 1940s to her death in 1977 she continued to write songs, but only the three Shakespeare songs were published in her lifetime (Lengnick, 1949). Knowledge of the rest of her songs has been limited almost entirely to a few friends who had manuscript copies.

The appearance in 1982 of a Meridian LP, *The Far Away Princess,* featuring 19 of her songs sung by Robert Tear, with Philip Ledger at the piano, gave a boost to her reputation and it was favourably reviewed; the recording was reissued as a Meridian cassette in 1992 KD 89018).

Madeleine Dring's music is traditional and diatonic, with vocal lines that are sympathetic and delightful harmonic subtleties in the keyboard parts. She could see no reason for writing in a style she found aurally incoherent, quoting William Walton's experience of having studied with Nadia Boulanger but nevertheless sticking to his own style thereafter. As Herbert Howells, her professor of composition at the RCM, put it: 'The only thing for a composer to do is to write honestly, to write what he or she wants to write'.

Madeleine Dring's gift was for assimilating what she liked from other composers and then 'producing something utterly original, something entirely the work of Madeleine Dring and none other', as James Harding said in a perceptive BBC broadcast about her in 1984.

Details of this series of five Dring song-volumes are given on the back cover. Where works have been published previously, the opportunity has been taken to correct mistakes. In some cases, too, songs have been transposed, to make them accessible to a wider body of singers.

Roger Lord © 1992

The cuckoo

Words by Shakespeare

Music by Madeleine Dring
(original key A♭)

When dai——sies pied and vi—o—lets blue And la—dy—smocks all sil—ver white And cuc——koo buds of yel——low hue Do paint the mea—dows

with ____ de - light, The cuc - koo then on ev' - ry tree ____

mocks mar - ried men, for thus sings he: Cuc - koo, Cuc -

- koo, Cuc - koo, Oh word __ of fear, Un - pleas ____ ing to ____ a ____

mar ____ ried ear! When

shep-herds pipe on oat - en straws And mer - ry larks are

plough - men's clocks, When tur — tles tread And rooks___ and daws, And

mai - dens bleach their sum - mer smocks, The cuc - koo then on

ev' - ry tree ___ mocks mar - ried men, For thus sings he:

It was a lover

Words by Shakespeare

Music by Madeleine Dring
(original key G)

Bet-ween the a – cres of the rye These

pret – ty coun – try folk would lie, these pret – ty coun – try folk would lie: ____

This ca – rol, This ca – rol, This ca – rol they be – gan that hour ____

Spring-time, the on-ly pret-ty ring-time, When birds do __ sing hey ding-a-ding

ding: Sweet lo _____ vers, Sweet lo _____

_____ vers, lo _____ vers, sweet lo _____ vers love the

Spring. _____

8va bassa

Take O take those lips away

Words by Shakespeare

Music by Madeleine Dring

Take O take those lips a-way That so sweet-ly were for-sworn,

And those eyes, the break of day Lights that do mis-lead the morn:

But my kiss-es Bring a-gain, Bring a-gain,

Bring a-gain Seals of love, but seal'd in vain,

Seal'd _____ in vain, _____ Seals_ of love,_ but seal'd _____ in _

vain!

Take   O   take__ those   lips   a - way   Take   O   take__ those   lips   a - way.

Under the greenwood tree

Words by Shakespeare

Music by Madeleine Dring

Come away, death

Words by Shakespeare

Music by Madeleine Dring

share it ... Not a flower, not a flower

sweet on my black cof - fin let there be strown

Not a friend, not a friend greet my poor corpse where my

bones shall be thrown.

A

thou-sand, thou-sand sighs to save Lay me, O where sad, true

lo - ver ne - ver find my grave *dim.*

Lay me, O where, sad, true lo-ver ne-ver

find my grave to weep there.

poco accel. *ten.*

Blow, blow thou winter wind

Words by Shakespeare

Music by Madeleine Dring

Blow, blow thou win-ter wind, Thou art not so un-kind as man's in-

-grat-i-tude

heigh - ho! the hol - ly! Then, heigh - ho! the hol - ly! This

life is most jol - ly

Freeze

freeze thou bit - ter sky, Thou dost not bite so nigh As ben - e -

Crabbed age and youth

Words by Shakespeare

Music by Madeleine Dring
(original keys G and A♭)

Age is weak and cold, Youth is wild and age is tame:

Age, I do ab-hor___ thee,

Youth, I do a-dore___ thee; O! my love, my love is young!___

Age, I do de-fy___ thee de - fy___ thee